Rejected Addresses: An Episode, In One Act

Emily S. Ford

In the interest of creating a more extensive selection of rare historical book reprints, we have chosen to reproduce this title even though it may possibly have occasional imperfections such as missing and blurred pages, missing text, poor pictures, markings, dark backgrounds and other reproduction issues beyond our control. Because this work is culturally important, we have made it available as a part of our commitment to protecting, preserving and promoting the world's literature. Thank you for your understanding.

# REJECTED ADDRESSES.

## AN EPISODE

IN ONE ACT.

BY

EMILY S. FORD.

ENTERED AT STATIONERS' HALL,

1882.

# REJECTED ADDRESSES.

SCENE.—*The Drawing-room, which should be arranged as æsthetically as possible with peacock feather fans, blue japanese jars, paintings of sun flowers, or lilies lying about.*

MED. (*at window*) How steady the rain! How fresh its gentle showers! Ah! would I could ever wander forth beside the purling brook, among the forest shades and bathe my feet among the tiny blades of grass all soaked in dew, and listen to the tiny throstle's note of joy. (*comes down*) But no, alas stern duty claims me. her finger cold and grave points to the crowded haunts of Cities' sites. Ah me! we must soon quit this lovely mansion; would I could say these halls of my Father's race, but alas! 'tis only a hired hall; for our lease, my sisters' and my own, comes to an end to-morrow, and ere a second sun can set we must return to all our varied duties. (*enter* PHILLIDA *carrying a cut lily*) Ha! Phillida, is't you? what shall we do when we return to Bloomsbury's sad streets and leave these leafy groves? (*seizes* PHIL's *hand*) Say, oh sister! will not sad grief seize your heart?

PHIL. (*disengaging her hand*) No, Medora, you have not yet achieved the age's highest point-culture! (*Raises lily and points to it*) You do not know how you should live.

MED. Don't I?

PHIL. No. You live too much on the mere outside of things. Now you should learn to shut your eyes to all unpleasantness. (*closes her eyes and stands wrapt in thought*). Then you need not ever know whether you are here or in Bloomsbury. (*they seat themselves*) Now look at me, I keep this blessed blossom ever near me. (*puts lily into blue flower pot and regards it ecstatically*) And in its most truly subtle preciousness I forget all base externals.

(*Enter* DIANA *with Tennis Racket and balls.*)

DIANA. Oh, I say this is awfully dull you know. Here have we been shut up for five weeks in this rainy hole and no one ever comes to see us; I do wish *someone* would call, if it were only the fat old squire.

MED. Don't speak of him, Diana; I hear his voice still ringing in my ears in those accents sharp and rough.

PHIL. And I can still see before me that most painful coat he wore; why it was, it really and most truly was—grey-check! Ah! (*sinks back in the chair overcome*)

DIANA. Well, it's true I was awfully glad to take this house for the summer, but then I must say I am tremendously pleased we are going to break up so soon. Only I wish *Med* and *Phil*

MED.  } *interrupting* { Med!!
PHIL. } { Phil!!

DIANA. Oh, bother, I do wish you'd let us take a house near the park, and then I could see my own friends and have fun. Why you WILL live near that horrid old British Museum I can't think, it's enough to give one a fit of the blues for a year only to go inside it for a minute.

MED. You forget, Diana, how it is the sacred purpose of my life to dedicate its days to the production of my work "Cæsario, or the heart-broken Pirate of the West."

PHIL. And oh, Diana! how *can* you speak in that frivolous manner of the temple where the last sad shadow of the Blessed Greeks may still be found in this philistian land.

DIANA. Oh, bother the pirates and the Greeks. Oh, joy, here comes Cherubina if she has only done her everlasting practising perhaps she'll be jolly and play tennis. (*enter* CHERUBINA *reading a Music score*) Cherubina, do let us play tennis in the hall.

CHER. Indeed, Diana, I don't think I can, I have so much to do, I have not yet finished the score of my cantata. Oh, Diana, you have no idea at all how fine the Adagio is, but listen how it goes. (*hums air and gets engrossed over it*)

DIANA. Ah there's *Pen* coming, I wish—

PHIL. Diana, *do* call her Penelope. It is a truly painful habit you have acquired of spoiling the purposeful intention of names by cutting them up into vague nothings.

CHER. (*ceasing humming*) Oh, Diana, you never listened, and I did want you to hear it, it is so fine. *Did* you hear it.

DIANA. No, I didn't really. But never mind. Here comes Pen.

PHIL. (*putting up her hands in deprecation*) Ah! again.

DIANA. Oh, well *Phillida* (*with emphasis*) *Penelope* if you wish. *I* don't care about *purposeful nothings*. (*with mimicking grandiloquence*)

(*Enter* PEN. *reading an open letter.*)

PEN. Something *so* interesting.

DIANA. Oh, What, What! (PHIL. *and* MED. *lean eagerly forward*)

PEN. A letter from Professor Stuffhead telling me what coach I had better get to prepare me for my little go. (MED. *and* PHIL. *lean back disappointed*).

DIANA. How tremendously slow; oh, dear, I'll see if it's still raining. (*goes up to window*) No, it's fine now. But, Oh, I say, there's no end of a row in the garden. There's Perkins bringing in a man leaning on his shoulder, who looks as if he had had a fall or hurt himself or something, and I believe, yes, no, yes it *is* a gentleman not just a *man* you know. Oh I'll go and see what it's all about. This *is* jolly, we've got a caller after all and he looks ever so much more fun than that fat old squire. (*Exit* DIANA *running.*)

CHER. Now, if a caller comes, I shan't get on with my cantata. Oh, how tiresome it is to have its thread broken just as it was coming. Penelope, let us go before this man comes, we shan't get any more work done to day, I fear.

PEN. No, I'm afraid not. (*exit* CHER *and* PEN)

MED. Suppose this stranger should turn out to be a poet, or—thrilling thought, a pirate in disguise; I'll go and watch from my window's height. (*exit* MED.)

PHIL. I do not like to have my outer harmony too suddenly broken. This man may wear a check. But no, the thought is too painful, for the present, I will retire with my blossom, so that at all events its quite too lovely harmony may keep my mind at rest. (*exit* PHIL. *with lily.*)

(*Enter* CAP. DEL. *leaning on* DIANA'S *arm.*)

CAP. DEL. I am afraid I hurt you, really, I'm so awfully sorry, upon my honour I am, I can't think how it was, but just as I was coming down the lane, I trod on a piece of orange peel some little beast of a boy had left there, and the road was greasy, you know, with this confounded shower, and I fell somehow; it's only now six weeks since I was laid up with rather an awkward sprain and now this has brought it on again, I suppose. (*seats himself in chair* DIANA *pushes to him.*) Really, you are very kind, Miss—ah—Miss?

DIANA. Oh, Di, that's my name, no end of a short name, but then it saves time, you know. (*seats herself on the arm of a chair and tosses up tennis balls taken from her pinafore pocket.*)

CAP. DEL. Is your time then so valuable, Miss Di?

DIANA. Well, you *are* stupid not to know that, why there's such a fearful heap of things to do, one never knows where to go next.

CAP. DEL. Oh I'm sure *you* can't have too much to do, Miss Di. Now if you were a poor wretch of a man and had to earn your own living and all that.

DIANA. (*interrupting him*) That's all *you* know about it, why anyone with half a head would understand that it's just because *I am* a girl, and just because I have *not* to earn my living that I have so much to do. At least you would if you knew my sisters.

CAP. DEL. Oh, then you have sisters, Miss Di.

DIANA. Oh, yes, any amount.

CAP. DEL. And how many may any amount be? If they are all as charming as yourself, Miss Di—

DIANA. (*interrupting him*) Oh, I say, stop that you know, I'd rather you'd tell me something jolly than spend your time in trying to make compliments.

CAP. DEL. Are not compliments jolly, Miss Di, when they are paid to yourself?

DIANA. Well, you see one gets such lots, one doesn't care for them.

CAP. DEL. Ah, then it's the *quantity*, not the *quality* you object to?

DIANA. Well, of course it makes *some* difference who makes them.

CAP. DEL. Ah, then after all it is not the *compliment* which displeases, but the complimen*ter*?

DIANA Ah, *now* I see it is *you* who like compliments. You want me to make out that *you* please me.

CAP. DEL. I am sure if I could get you to "make out" any such delightful thing, it would be immensely pleasing to me, Miss Di.

DIANA. Then you must be very amusing and tell me a lot of things. Oh, by-the-by (*drops her voice confidentially*) *do* you know (*he moves nearer and pulls his foot with his hand after him, she breaks off on seeing his movement*) but you are sure you are quite comfortable? Oh dear, what a dolt I am. See you should have that foot raised, and there's no footstool, I'll go and fetch one. (*exit* DIANA.)

CAP. DEL. By jove, she's charming, I say I must look out. There's a dreadful habit I've got, and that is proposing to all the girls I meet, and the worst of it is, that they all accept me;

it's only two months since I was laid up with this ridiculous ankle, and then I know I left the house I was staying in full of broken hearts, and all that sort of thing; well, it was hard on a fellow, it really was, but what was I to do? when a man has to lie all day on a sofa, and charming girls get rugs, hand tea, look sorry, and speak sadly, &c. &c., why, what can a fellow do but say he likes it, and how can he better say he likes it than by asking the charming girls to get rugs and hand tea for him *for ever?* I don't *mean* to ask, but they all take it so, and well,—I rather flatter myself I *do* make an impression,—in fact,—I don't think I'm altogether what you might call disagreeable, in fact, I should call myself on the whole fascinating; yes, I don't think that is going it too strong, I don't indeed. But it's an awful thought "*any amount*" of sisters; why who knows but I might get engaged to them all at once. Well, I suppose I must resign myself to it, if it *does* come, (*moving seems to hurt his foot*) but I can't resign myself to this foot, though it's not so bad but if Miss Di. were not so charming I could go away at once. Oh, here she comes, Miss No. 1. any amount.

(*Enter* DIANA *with the footstool.*)

DIANA. Here's a footstool (*puts it under his foot*) Oh, what's *your* name by-the-bye?

CAP. DEL. Captain Delaville, Miss Di.

DIANA. Ah, then you're army, that's how *you* earn your living. I say, do you know cousin Frank? he's army too, you know.

CAP. DEL. Oh, I know him, he's a nice fellow, isn't he?

DIANA. *Of course* he is awfully nice.

CAP. DEL. Rather short, isn't he?

DIANA. Oh *dear* no, he's ever so tall.

CAP. DEL. Then that's he, he's dark, isn't he? (*watches* DI. *carefully, she shakes her head*) At least in a way.

DIANA. Well, he's sort of neither you know.

CAP. DEL. That's Frank to a T.

DIANA. Oh, then you *do* know him?

CAP. DEL. Perfectly, see him every day of my life. (*aside*) I never saw him in my life. *Must* have wanted to know something about this Cousin Frank, when she began, "do you know?" (*sentimentally*) what *did* you want to know Miss Di. just before you went out of the room to fetch the footstool, don't you remember you said, "now do you know?"

DIANA. Oh, yes, and I *do* want to know, oh, so much, do tell me, but (*sadly*) I'm afraid you won't know, no one *ever* does, and I have so often longed and longed to hear.

Cap. Del. Tell me, Miss Di. don't fear to confide in me. (*aside*) Now she's going to tell me the secret of her life, it's the way they always do.

Diana. Well, but after all it's hardly worth while to ask *you*.

Cap. Del. Oh, Miss Di. you pain me, I entreat you to have no fear, but tell, only tell me plainly.

Diana. Oh well, if you *really* wish to know.

Cap. Del. I do indeed, upon my honour I do.

Diana. It's just this, where had I better go, if I want to get the very best bull terrier.

Cap. Del. Really, I—er—really, I hardly know, I can't tell.

Diana. What a sell, I thought you'd be sure to know.

Cap. Del. (*aside*) After all it's rather a relief it's not about Cousin Frank. I didn't see why on earth she should have been interested in him. Shows her sense not to care about him. (*aloud*) So you are interested in dogs, Miss Di. Is *that* what makes you so busy?

Diana Oh, dear no, dogs are only one item. There's— hunting when one gets the chance, and there's—but oh never mind this, let us talk of something else, something *really* interesting this time.

Cap. Del. But really, I don't quite know what is—"interesting," for I talked about yourself a little time ago, and you voted *that* dull. I don't know what *can* be interesting after that.

Diana Oh, there are plenty of things to talk about. Let me see, let us—I know—let us talk about *you*, at all events it's something new.

Cap Del. (*aside*) Something new, *that's* all I am, is it? (*aloud*) I am sure for me to be talked about by so charming a young lady as yourself would indeed be interesting.

Diana Oh, bother, I told you before not to pay compliments. Tell me how you like earning your living and all that you know. Is it dull?

Cap. Del. Beastly dull, nothing more dull under the sun. There's nothing *new* in it either. It's dull as ditch-water.

Diana Why at all events there would be the—excitement of thinking whether you did earn it or not.

Cap. Del. A very pleasing excitement when you *don't* earn it, that I can tell you.

Diana Oh, but anything is fun if you mean only to have fun always and not mind things.

Cap. Del. (*aside*) What a jolly girl; always finds fun; suppose I *do* ask her after all? I suppose she'd find that fun.

DIANA. Now then something else. Be quick. Amuse me.

CAP. DEL. Well, I *was* going to say.

DIANA. What? quick, speak out.

CAP. DEL. Well, suppose you *do* earn your living, that is, I mean suppose that I do, that is, suppose we earn it together?

DIANA. But I don't understand.

CAP. DEL. Well you see, you like fun, don't you?

DIANA. I said so before.

CAP. DEL. Well, so do I.

DIANA. Then we both do. (*bell rings*) Oh, that is Tibbs, I know it is, he was to call and tell me what I must do about sending Brown Bess up to town. My hunter you know. But, never mind about all that, I *must* go and see him myself, servants always make such muddles, (*runs to door and stops*) but I'll come back and then we'll talk it over. I don't know what you mean, but I daresay we shall agree. (*exit* DI.)

CAP. DEL. Well, if that isn't accepting, I don't know what is; of course she knew what I meant. A girl always knows when a fellow's proposing to her. Besides she said we should agree and so of course that was her way of saying yes. No doubt she has made up all that about Tibbs or some one, to hide her feelings. I declare I feel quite affected myself, (*wipes his eyes with handkerchief*) The thing is, do I feel *pleased*? I suppose a fellow ought to feel pleased under the circumstances. But somehow now when I think it over, I begin to feel I have been just a little precipitate. Might have gone it a little slower. But the fact is, I really do feel rather afraid of the girl. Comes down on one so quick. I don't like that way of saying "quick" "speak out." Hollo! here's No. 2, suppose I tell her about No. 1. Really I wish I had seen her first.

(*Enter* CHERUBINA. *Seats herself.*)

CHER. Di tells me you are feeling better. I hope it is so?

CAP. DEL. (*aside*) Of course she thinks me better when she has—accepted me. That proves she *has* accepted me. (*aloud*) Yes, I am better, you see a fall like that does give one a shock.

CHER. No doubt. Just like a false note in the middle of a scherzo. It's very bad, very.

CAP. DEL. Well, I don't know about the—er—skirts—oh but I *do* about the fall.

CHER. Of course you like music?

CAP. DEL. Oh yes, it's very jolly sometimes.

CHER. I think *jolly* is hardly the word to apply to Wagner's divine compositions.

CAP. DEL. Isn't it? well, you know I was thinking of "Nancy Lee" awfully good tune, that, you know.

CHER. I don't care for tunes.

CAP. DEL. How odd: I thought you liked music? "Nancy Lee" is no end of a song you know. (*sings*)

"Of all the wives as e'er you know
Yeo ho lads, yeo ho.
There's none like Nancy Lee I trow
Yeo ho lads, yeo ho."

(CHER. *regards him first with horror, then puts her hands over her ears*) It is fine, it really is.

CHER. I don't call songs music.

CAP. DEL. What are they, then?

CHER. Oh assemblages of *merely* pleasing sounds.

CAP DEL. Isn't *that* music.

CHER. Oh, no. Music is the—But first, of course you know—the difference between harmony and melody.

CAP. DEL. Oh, Oh,—of course. (*aside*) This is far enough off No. 1. But she looks so interesting I don't mind, though what she means, I haven't an idea.

CHER. Well then, having founded our definition of these two fundamental principles, we might proceed to a rigid scrutiny of the more complex form in which the musical idea seeks to find expression for itself. Do you know what it is which most deeply interests me at present.

CAP. DEL. No, indeed, I don't. But upon my honour there is nothing else I would rather know.

CHER. I'll tell you, but remember, I have never told a soul before. This is a profound secret.

CAP. DEL. I will not forget. (*aside*) So she entrusts me with the secret of her life. I knew it would be so. I shall have to propose to her too, it is my fate. (*aloud*) Your secret, Miss —er—Miss?

CHER. Oh, Cherubina, but pray attend. (*gazes into space*) Oh, I see it clearly the sonata, it is true, expresses the more concentrated form of the musical idea, and the symphony the more extended form. Now I am, don't be surprised, don't be too much excited—but—I am writing a cantata.

CAP. DEL. Bless my soul: are you indeed? (*aside*) I suppose she expects me to be surprised.

CHER. But it is *not* a cantata. I *call* it so to the outer world, but I have another yet undecided name for it.

CAP. DEL. Indeed?

CHER. You see the world, the musical world, that is, and of course no one out of that counts for anything —

CAP. DEL. Of course not. That is, Miss Cherubina, you include *me* in the musical world, do you not?

CHER. Oh, how you interrupt, what *does* that matter.

CAP. DEL. I assure you it matters a great deal, pray do not be so cruel as to leave me out in the cold altogether. I assure you *I love* music.

CHER. But you like *tunes*.

CAP. DEL. Oh, that was a mistake. I did *once*. I've outgrown them.

CHER. But you seem to like *songs*.

CAP. DEL. With you, Miss Cherubina, to teach me I really think I might outgrow *them* too.

CHER. Well, perhaps you might, but this is wandering from the point, indeed you interrupt me very much, and I have not told you my secret.

CAP. DEL. Indeed I beg your pardon, Miss Cherubina, I thought you had when you said you were writing something.

CHER. Oh, but that is not all, the rest is *very* exciting.

CAP. DEL. I am all excitement. (*aside*) I must let her have her head, I suppose, and she looks so charming when she goes into raptures I must forgive her that I can't understand what she is driving at.

CHER. Now you really *must* listen (*they draw their chairs closer*) The musical world needs another vehicle in which to express its ideas—ideas of the future, I mean—those of the past are worthless. What do we care now for Mozart? Mere tunes, I assure you. Beethoven? well, he was all very well you know, he meant well. But with such poor channels in which to express his ideas—well, what could you expect, you know?

CAP. DEL What indeed!

CHER. As I say, poor Beethoven: the *new* world needs something more. It need's a Wagner of the future. A master mind who shall find a form semi-sonata, semi-symphony, and not at all cantata. *I* seek to find that form.

CAP. DEL. Do you indeed!

CHER. Yes. *That* is my secret. Does it not thrill you? It does me. You do not know what a privilege you have in sitting by me.

CAP. DEL. Upon my soul I do. I could sit here for ever. I could indeed.

CHER. Ah, perhaps there is some hope for you after all·

Now you have had the privilege of hearing me *speak*, me, who one day may be a follower of the great new composer, the future Wagner of the future. Now, if you like, before I leave the room, you may—shake hands with me—that in future years you may recal this proud moment and say, she, the disciple of the future, the Wagner of the future, gave me her hand; here is my hand. (*rises and holds it out to him*) Take it; (*he takes it.*)

CAP. DEL. I do with pleasure. (*exit* CHERUBINA) Well, *she's* done it this time, not me, for when a lady offers you her hand, there is only one meaning to be put upon it. I said it was my fate. Two already in half an hour, how many more may there be? Heavens! here's No. 3. I can't face her, I can't indeed. (*hides his face in his hands. Enter* MEDORA.)

MED. (*creeps in on tiptoe, carefully watching* CAPTAIN DELAVILLE) Is he a pirate or is he not? I will discover (*sees his face hid*) Ha! weeping, that looks well. I begin to hope. Alas poor stranger, why do you weep: fear no harm. No danger shall befall you within these halls of my—ahem—of my fatherland. Speak, only speak to me.

CAP. DEL. (*with head still averted*) Madam, what *can* I say?

MED. No, gentle sir, after the surging billow's storm you must needs require rest for your scattered wits.

CAP. DEL. (*starting*) Shattered wits be hanged: does the girl think I am mad!

MED. Nay, do not start, you fain would seek rest. (*aside*) No, he didn't answer to my allusion to the sea, he only muttered to himself, I daresay he wished to keep it a secret that he is a pirate. I won't speak too openly of it.

CAP. DEL. (*perplexed*) Your sisters and yourself are very— (*tries hard to find a word*) hospitable

MED. I trust we are. It would ill become those with whom the fine arts have found a home to treat the *Homeless* stranger with contempt.

CAP. DEL. (*aside*) Can she know about my position to No. 1 and No. 2? I will try and find out. (*aloud*) You see Miss—er—Miss?

MED. Medora is my name, *Captain* Delaville. I hear it is *Captain* Delaville to whom I speak.

CAP. DEL. It is, you see, Miss Medora, it is this way. (*stops hesitatingly.*)

MED. (*aside*) He must be in disguise, it is not his real name. I see it all now. (*aloud*) Do not speak, do not try to tell that which I know full well is too painful to tell.

Cap. Del. (*aside*) She *must* know. (*aloud*) So, Miss Medora, it is you whom your sisters make the confidante of their troubles, that is, I mean their happiness.

Med. They do. I am safe.

    Safe as lethean stream,
    Whose waters once you drink, shall steep
    Your senses in forgetfulness, whose dusky beam
    Into your soul with shadows dark shall creep.

Listen, Captain. It is a secret, you know, remember that.

Cap. Del. (*aside*) Another secret! what possesses them to tell me their secrets. (*aloud*) All right, fire away! I'll listen.

Med. (*aside*) "Fire away!" a truly piratic expression. He's got into it by habit. (*aloud*) My secret is, I am writing a poem which shall convince the world the spirit of Byron still lives. I'll read some to you. (*gets out* M.S.S.) (*aside*) Now I'll find the part describing Cæsario, and I'll watch him as I read. (*reads*)

    Dost see that mighty brow, that falcon eye?
    Dost see all this, and then dost think that I
    Could choose another, when this pirate fair
    Stands here, and gazes forth with lucent gaze
    Fixed on the past, and all its happy days.

Now is not that fine.

Cap. Del. Magnificent. (*aside*) I haven't an idea what it's about.

Med. (*aside*) He seems interested. Soft, Captain.

Cap. Del. Miss Medora!

Med. Tell me truly, I swear I'll not reveal it, only tell me truly.

Cap. Del. (*aside faintly*) Now it's coming. (*aloud*) Oh anything.

Med. Are you?—hush—(*gets up and searches the room*) no one is listening, no one sees or hears. Now speak the truth.

    Brave Captain, tell me true I pray,
      Ah, tell me true or die,
    This answer make, now to me say
      The truth, and if I sigh,
    Forget nor think again of me
      For if a pirate be not thou,
    I tell thee fair I'll forget thee
      So tell me true, and tell me now.

Cap. Del. (*aside*) She must be mad, my deceit has driven her mad, and now she's asking me to marry her, I'm sure she is, she can't mean anything else, because she doesn't know what else to do. I daren't refuse her or she'll stab me, and I can't get to the bell, I don't know where it is, I'll accept her, there's nothing else for it. (*aloud*) Yes, Lady, Yes.

MED. (*starting and clasping her hands*) Ah! 'tis true then, I have at last found a pirate on which to mould my "Cæsario," how fortunate; I feared they were all extinct—I promise *never* to reveal.

CAP. DEL. Thanks (*aside*) I hope she won't, seeing she's No. 3. Heavens! here's No. 4, my brain is going.

*Enter* PHILLIDA *with Lily.*

MED. I'll go, it may excite suspicion, remember *silence*. (*Exit* MEDORA.)

PHIL. (*seating herself*) I really could not let you remain so long *alone* with my sister, Captain Delaville; Diana tells me you are Captain Delaville.

CAP. DEL. (*aside*) Then my suspicions are true, Medora is mad, I've been in danger of my life. (*aloud*) And why Miss—er—Miss?

PHIL. Oh, Phillida.

CAP. DEL. Why should I not remain alone with your sister, Miss Phillida?

PHIL. Oh, she has such erroneous views, poor Medora.

CAP. DEL. (*eagerly*) Ah!

PHIL. Yes, she belongs to a bygone age, she knows nothing of culture.

CAP. DEL. You mean she's—eccentric.

PHIL. Oh, dear no, she's just like everybody else, you know. *That* is her fault.

CAP. DEL. (*aside*) Then she's *not* mad, and I needn't have accepted her; well she is very pretty.

PHIL. Now I should like, you know, to set all your views straight again, I really should.

CAP. DEL. Madam, I am all attention, I assure you to be taught by so charming a young lady as yourself would be happiness.

PHIL. Now, this is truly intense to find a nature so easily led. There is still hope for you, I assure you there is; you cannot be altogether the degenerate Philistine one meets so often, oh so quite too often, and who is, I grieve to say an utterly hopeless being. I daresay you'll think I talk a great deal, but I assure you I don't often. Talking is a mistake.

CAP. DEL. It is indeed.

PHIL. But it is right when the proper moment comes to scatter the good seed, and you, I believe, have arrived at that moment when the initiation into the higher life is possible, just possible. To begin with then—

CAP. DEL. (*interrupting*) Yes, but your sister, you were going to speak of her, I think.

PHIL. Ah, yes, it is well you have recalled me to myself I am apt to wander. In these days we inherit not too much intellect, oh, no. But so quite too much feeling.

CAP. DEL. (*aside*) By jove, she's amusing, if I only knew what she was talking about; I'll bring her back again. (*aloud*). Well, but your sister?

PHIL. Ah, yes, thanks again. No doubt she quoted *verses*— *Rhymes*. (*with contemptuous emphasis*) to you.

CAP. DEL. I must say she did.

PHIL. Do not trust her. (CAP. DEL. *starts eagerly*) Her theory of *Art* (*he falls back languidly*) is all one utter mistake, from beginning to end; why I know you'll not believe me, but she really and truly reads Byron still, and ha, ha —(*laughs languidly*) but, only it is so much, so quite too absurd, believes he is a *poet*, I knew you would not believe me, but it is a sad truth. Now if you knew how consummately superior *our* school is, the school of the future of course I mean, how supremely more subtle in its meaning, how distinctly more precious in its phrases—I will quote from one author only, not myself, I don't compose,—that is to say, the many, the infinitely many, great poems, which I have felt so often are still here, (*pointing to her head*) and here they will remain, because you know to think is *enough*, to write, to speak, to act, to give *any* outer expression to the inner blessed idea, is—*vulgar*—it is against the principles of my school *ever* to compose.

CAP. DEL. But, my dear young lady, how does anyone know you exist?

PHIL. But, my dear Captain, what *does* that signify? if we are, why—we are.

CAP. DEL. True.

PHIL. I will do no more than quote my author, and then I know you will feel the higher life has began.

"I asked of the darkness, art thou dark?
I asked of my soul, art thou thyself?
Did they reply? Ah, did they then?
That darkness dark, that spirit mine."

Now is not that consummately utter?

Cap. Del. It—er—it does not rhyme!
Phil. What then?
Cap. Del. I don't quite understand it.
Phil. To think that that can signify shows you are still in quite outermost darkness; if once a precious poet has breathed forth the consummate stanza, what does rhyme matter, to what purpose is the common reason of the common man?
Cap. Del. (*aside*) I really should like to make the conversation a little more personal. (*aloud*) May I ask, Miss Phillida, if you are fond of gardening? You seem to care for flowers, judging by your devotion to that lily.
Phil There is not enough purposeful beauty in gardening for me to care to pursue it. But in the blessed harmony of this lily I ever restore my mind.
Cap. Del. May I keep that lily, Miss Phillida, as a remembrance of my initiation into the higher life.
Phil. Then you must scan its fair lines and learn its sweet colours by heart, and forget them not. Take it, keep it—it is valueless in itself, but it means, Oh, certainly, it means such depths of untold meaning (*gives him flower and rises*) You must excuse me, indeed you must, this subject is always one which is too utter for me, I must retire. (*exit* Phil.)
Cap. Del. (*drops flower on floor*) Well, really, I believe I've done it again, though whether it was she or I who did it first I don't know, I didn't mean it altogether when I asked her for the flower, but she thought I did, and so it comes to the same thing. However, *she's* quite serious, and seemed quite overcome. I'd better go now at once. Ah! here's another of them, I can't escape.

(*Enter* Pen, *with pile of books, and seats herself.*)

Pen. Are you one of those people whose mental faculties are sharpened by bodily illness, or do you belong to that class which succumbs mentally when physical conditions are not favourable?
Cap. Del. I really don't know. I don't feel conscious of much mental faculty at any time.
Pen. Ah, that is hardly the answer I should have expected from you. I should have thought from your appearance that you indulged in self-analysis, however, I have not come to any conclusion as yet as to the connexion between mind and body. However, I think, or I perceive, or rather I am aware from past experience that such subjects do not interest a mind not inherently scientific in its tendencies.

Cap. Del. I assure you Miss—er—Miss.?
Pen. Oh, Penelope.
Cap. Del. I assure you, Miss Penelope, anything that interests *you* would have a profound interest for *me*.
Pen. Ah! compliments. I see you are one of those people who pay compliments, you belong to that class evidently. Well I must say I don't belong to that section of the human race who experience any favourable emotion from that form of address. How would you define a compliment?
Cap. Del. Well, I might say,—perhaps I should call it—a sort of homage paid to the attractive.
Pen. That is no definition, however I will not be socratic and push the love of definition too far. Socrates was all very well in his way, but he was not the sort of person *I* should have cared to have much to do with, he tended too much to depress the energy of those who seek to pursue original research.
Cap Del. Are *you* indulging in original research, Miss Penelope? I should like to help in that original research.
Pen. Oh, I have devoted my life to science.
Cap. Del. Happy science.
Pen. But alas, *Scientia longa, vita brevis est.*
Cap. Del. Ah! Yes.
Pen. Suppose I read aloud to you—something light. I have got Mill's Logic and Spencer's Psychology, which would you prefer?
Cap. Del. I assure you I would rather hear your own sentiments and *talk* Miss Penelope —hear you talk about—well —(Pen. *waits eagerly*) science.
Pen. This *is* interesting. Now if people would always indulge in rational conversation how much might be elicited.
Cap. Del. How much, indeed!
Pen. For instance, if you would consent to an hour's talk every day, how much we might get through; of course we should begin with the more elementary part of sociology.
Cap. Del. Miss Penelope, I assure you I would gladly converse with you every day of my life. (*aside*) If that is not putting it neatly, I don't know what is.
Pen. This is wonderful in a person of your capacity. I assure you there is hope for you. But I will leave you now to your reflections, it is never well to talk much, and as all my sisters have conversed with you, I think you have had enough for the present. And you will, I am sure, excuse us till lunch time as we are all so busy. We lunch at one. (*Exit* Pen.)
Cap. Del. "Enough for the present!" I should rather think

I have. That's No. 5! for she has accepted me too, she said there was hope for me. Yes, it is too true, and I did it myself this time. Let me see she said "all my sisters," then there are no more. Well I've gone it strong this time, I have indeed, I'll not stay another instant. I'll—I'll—I don't know, stop—I'll—my ankle's nothing. I can't meet the whole five at once, I'll go to the Inn and I'll leave a note saying, I've got a telegram from my Great Aunt saying she's dead. No, that won't do, I must say I've got a telegram saying she's dead, and I must go home at once. But no, I must see them again, that charming Di, (*sighs*) that fascinating Cherubina, that beautiful, though mad, Medora, that wonderful Phillida, that most wonderful Penelope. (*gets up*) Yes, I'll try to get a private interview with each, and then, (*sits down to writing table and writes*) now here goes "Dear ladies, I regret that sudden intelligence of the loss of my Great Aunt obliges me to leave you somewhat suddenly, and stern duty calls me to the impoverished Halls of my Father's race." I think that's rather fine about stern duty and impoverished halls. Now how shall I end, yours affectionately? No, yours ever? well, no not to all. Yours very sincerely, very truly, faithfully, yes faithfully R. C. DELAVILLE" I'll address it "to my charming hostesses" and I'll leave it on the chair I have been sitting on. Then I'll write separate notes to each of them, and I'll make them all alike, it'll save time. (*takes five sheets of paper and writes on each in succession the following letter*) "Most charming Di" (*refers to second sheet*) "Medora" (*to third sheet*) "Cherubina" (*to fourth sheet*) "Phillida" (*to fifth sheet*) "Penelope" (*and so through the letter*) "I cannot leave these halls without seeing you again to bid a long farewell; you know why I must say that farewell alone. A sad domestic affliction compels me to withdraw myself from your presence, most charming Di, Medora, Cherubina, Phillida, Penelope; ere long I will return to claim that lovely hand which you have bestowed upon me. Your devoted, R. C. DELAVILLE." Now I'll put them in various corners and I'll trust they'll each find the right one, and as they are so fond of secrets they won't tell each other. I'll go now or they'll find me. (*exit* DELAVILLE. *enter* DI.) Oh, he's gone (*finds note*) and left a note "to my charming hostesses" Here, sisters, he's gone (*enter* MED.) let us open this note. (*opens*)

MED. (*aside*) A note from the pirate, he has been secretly ordered off to join his ship. (*aloud*) Read it, Diana, read it.

DIANA. (*reads*) "Dear Ladies, I regret that sudden intelligence of the loss of my Great Aunt obliges me to leave you somewhat suddenly, and stern duty calls me to the impoverished halls of my father's race. Yours faithfully, R. C. DELAVILLE."

MED. (*shewing two notes*) Why it's the same handwriting as these two notes I found, one in the umbrella stand and one in the keyhole of the front door; see, one is addressed "to Miss Medora" let us peruse it together. (*reads*) "Most charming Medora, I cannot leave these halls without seeing you again to bid a long farewell. You know why I must say that farewell alone. A sad domestic affliction compels me to withdraw myself from your presence, most charming Medora, ere long I will return to claim that lovely hand which you have bestowed upon me. Your devoted DELAVILLE." What *can* he mean?

DIANA What indeed, and this other (*takes the other note from* MED.) is directed to me. (*reads*) "To Miss Di. Most charming Di, I cannot leave these halls without seeing you again to bid a long farewell. You know why I must say that farewell alone. A sad domestic affliction compels me to withdraw myself from your presence, most charming Di, ere long I will return to claim that lovely hand which you have bestowed upon me. Your devoted R. C. DELAVILLE." I say, how slow to write both alike. (*enter* PHIL.)

PHIL. What *can* be the purport of this, I found it (*shakes it carefully*) under the door mat. (*reads*) "Most charming Phillida."

MED. Medora!

DIANA. Di! (MED. *and* DIANA *point to their letters.*)

PHIL. (*stares in surprise and while reading aloud keeps looking at theirs*) "I cannot leave these halls without seeing you again to bid you a long farewell. You know why I must say that farewell alone. A sad domestic affliction compels me to withdraw myself from your presence, most charming Phillida, ere long I will return to claim that lovely hand which you have bestowed upon me. Your devoted R. C. DELAVILLE."

DIANA. How awfully odd!

MED. How truly strange!

PHIL. How quaint! (*enter* CHER.)

CHER. Just listen to this, I found it in the racket press. (*reads*) "Most charming Cherubina"

PHIL. Phillida!

MED. Medora!
DIANA. Di! (PHIL. MED. *and* DIANA *show their letters to* CHER. *she pushes them aside.*)
CHER. No, No, Cherubina "I cannot leave these halls without seeing you again"
PHIL. "Seeing you again" (*showing her letter which* CHER. *again pushes away.*)
CHER. "To bid a long farewell"
MED. "A long farewell" (*shows her letter,* CHER. *refuses to look*)
CHER. "A sad domestic affliction compels me to withdraw myself from your presence, most charming Cherubina."
DIANA. Di!
PHIL. Phillida!
MED. Medora (*all show their letters in turn.*)
CHER. "Ere long I will return to claim that lovely hand which you have bestowed upon me."
DIANA, PHIL. MED. (*together*) "You have bestowed upon me."
    (CHER. *looks at them all in turn*).
CHER. "Your devoted R. C. DELAVILLE."
PHIL. How quite too funny (*enter* PENELOPE.)
PEN. I must say this is one of the strangest phenomena I have ever come across. I saw this in the card basket. Can you explain it?
DIANA. What another of them!
PHIL. How utterly curious.
PEN. (*reads*) Most charming Penelope.
CHER. Cherubina.
PHIL. Phillida.
MED. Medora.
DIANA. Di.
(*They all show them in turn. They stand in a row in front of the foot-lights.*
CHER. PHIL. MED. DI. (*together*) I cannot leave these halls without seeing you again to bid a long farewell. You know why I must say that farewell alone, a sad domestic affliction compels me to withdraw myself from your presence, most charming—(*each substitutes her own name*) ere long I will return to claim that lovely hand—(*each raises her left hand and gazes admiringly on it*) which you have bestowed upon me. Your devoted, R. C. DELAVILLE.
PEN. (*keeps referring her letter to theirs in astonishment.*)

DIANA. Oh, heavens, what can it mean!
CHER. Well, it *is* odd. It might make a good idea for an opera.
PHIL. No Cherubina, you forget the opera— is—*vulgar*.
CHER. Well, *perhaps* it *is* out of date.
PEN. It is certainly rather remarkable. But it now remains for us to elucidate the matter; let us begin at once. The first point must be to consider what cause can have led this individual to express such curious sentiments; next, are those sentiments grounded on truth, or are they the mere baseless figments of an overheated imagination?
MED. The baseless fabric of a *dream* which fled like summer's breath.
DIANA. Shut up, Med., let's talk it out. My own opinion is, that somehow or other he thinks he's engaged to all of us at once.
CHER. *Quite* Operatic!
PEN. And how could he arrive at the conclusion; I hardly see on what ground he based his premises.
DIANA. I have it! He said we'd earn our living together, and I said I'd think about it.
CHER. Ah, now I remember; I said I would shake hands with him because I had told him my secret. You all know my secret?
DIANA. Oh, yes. we all know. I'm sure, Cherubina, it's not a secret now, I'd give up having it if I were you; it's getting slow.
CHER. Remember, Diana, *True* music must ever be for the *few* not for the many.
PHIL. That's a quite too supremely precious truth.
MED. Ah! now *I* recall. He took my verses addressed to a pirate to mean himself. How wildly unfortunate.
PHIL. How truly quaint! I gave him a flower to initiate him into the higher life. I see he is a Philistine after all. How sorrowful!
PEN. But this is very remarkable. There is stuff in it to make an essay on some curious tendencies of the masculine mind to exaggerate external phenomena. He has misunderstood my remark about rational conversation.
DIANA. I suppose he means us to toss up who is to have him; to be one of five makes one feel no end small.
PHIL. It is hardly what I think one would call good form.
CHER. Altogether out of tune, I should say.
DIANA. Well, what's to be done?
MED. Yes, *that* is the question.

CHER. Let us think it over (*they all retire to back and stand a few instants in contemplative attitudes.*)

MED, Let us swear eternal vengeance (*they all advance hand in hand to foot-lights and frown.*)

ALL Yes, yes.

DIANA. Let us give him a regular good blowing-up.

CHER. A sort of finale with wind instruments.

MED. The savage eyes of Nemesis shall o'er him gloat.

PEN. Let us all write and refuse him in the same terms just like his letter.

DIANA No, no, because then he'll think it's spite, green-eyed jealousy and all that sort of thing.

PHIL. Yes, don't let him know we have found out he has written to us all.

MED. That still shall remain a deep, mysterious secret.

ALL. (*clasping hands and advancing dramatically to foot-lights in a solemn whisper*) Yes!

DIANA. Look here! Let us each see him separately and tell him we have changed our minds.

ALL. Yes, yes. (*a ring is heard outside*)

CHER. He's coming, now quick! quick! Let us all go out but you, Di, you stay here.

ALL. Yes, yes. (*exeunt all but Di. Enter Cap. Del.*)

CAP. DEL. Oh, charming Miss Di.—

DIANA Don't you compliment me, Sir, I told you years ago I was engaged to cousin Frank.

CAP. DEL. You didn't.

DIANA I did. Or if I didn't exactly tell you I said he was awfully nice, and it's the same thing in a way. (*exit Di. Cap. Del. walks away from the door; enter Cher. Cap Del. in walking up and down comes full on Cher.*)

CAP. DEL. Oh, charming Miss Cherubina—

CHER. No, no, you do not love, nay you do not even *know* what true love is. You like tunes, you like songs. True music knows neither tunes nor songs. The future Wagner of the future is to you *but* future. You live in the past, or, still worse in the present. You have no soul; in short you are not of the musical world therefore you count for nothing (*exit Cher. Enter Med., Cap. Del. encounters her in the same manner as he encountered Cher.*

CAP. DEL. Oh, charming Miss Medora.

MED. What, did you not understand, do you not know, that never, never will I bend the heart to aught save a pirate. You are not one, you did deceive me, Oh hideous monster of deceit.

CAP. DEL. Hideous! I say now Miss Medora, don't you think that going it rather strong? You don't think I'm hideous, now do you really?

MED. Speak not before me. Utter not one sound. Quail, Oh man before me, for with the thunders of my voice I do proclaim you to be false, *false*, deceitful, cowardly and base. You told me in one breath you were a pirate. Now do you deny it? Is not this true? Speak wretch, are you or are you not a pirate?

CAP. DEL. Well, to speak the truth—

MED. (*interrupting*) Yes, speak the truth at last,
  At last, Oh, man, the truth do tell.
  And tremble now, thy hour is near
  And try thou, e'er so bravely well
  To face me, know thy foe is here.

*Are* you a pirate

CAP. DEL. No, I can't say I am.

MED. Attempt it not, or perjured thou shalt fall,
  And never on truth's icy height shalt rise at all.

(*exit* MED.)

CAP. DEL. (*stands with his back to the door. Enter* PHIL.)

PHIL. Well!

CAP. DEL. (*starting and turning round*) I asked you to meet me, I—I—I—

PHIL. How quaint.

CAP. DEL. I wish to say good-bye.

PHIL. How utterly utter.

CAP. DEL. I wanted to know if—if—

PHIL. Have you kept my blossom? (CAP. DEL. *begins searching about the room*) I want to know if you have preserved its pristine harmony.

CAP. DEL. I'm afraid I've lost it. Ah, here it is (*picks up flower all crushed and hands it to* PHIL.)

PHIL. Ah! (*takes flower with tips of her fingers and instantly drops it between them on the floor*) I see you *are* a Philistine after all. No more need be said. (*exit* PHIL. *Enter* PEN.)

CAP. DEL. Ah you've come to give me an hour's conversation.

PEN. No, I based my conclusion on false premises. You gave me to understand that rational conversation was what you liked, I have never allowed myself to indulge in *any* but rational conversation. Having ascertained that it is not the ultimate aim of your united forces, I do not consider the subject is worthy of any further consideration. (*exit* Pen.)

Cap. Del. Talk about leaving broken hearts I don't see any *here* I'm sure—in fact, in fact—I think, I really do think *I have* a heart, and it has been five times broken in one day, nay in one hour. Fair ladies, you have this day revenged your sisters. (*Takes up his hat and turns as if going, then walks up to the foot-lights.*)

  The play is o'er,
  There is no more,
I'm sure it's quite enough
  I'm left alone,
  I'm turned to stone,
On me they were most rough.

  I fear you'll be,
  As sad as me,
And quite as glad to go;
  Well, never mind
  Though fate's unkind,
One never should *say* so.

(*Enter* Di. *advances to foot-lights.*)

Di. Do say now that our play is done,
  It's not been *very* slow,
Quick, do speak out, and say some fun
You've found; I hope it's so.
  I've been most awfully afraid,
  'Twould be no go at all,
I thought our boldness would be paid,
  By feeling very small.

(*Enter* Cher.)

Cher. When first we planned this trifling little play,
What throbs of fright most harsh I cannot say,
Did swiftly come into my dreary, troubled mind,
Like sound of winter's strong and stormy wind,
I looked into the future then with curious eye,
I tried to read the meaning of its mystic sigh,
Alas, its chords were sad, I dare not listen long,
Oh, tell me that its note was false, and I was wrong.

(*Enter* Med. *comes to foot-lights.*)

Med. 'Tis true *my* heart did quickly beat,
  More swiftly came my fears,
Than sounds of ocean waves most sweet

Like showers fell my tears.
Forgive these tears, and *do* shed some,
Since to a close our play has come.

Oh, can it be that in your midst, (*pointing to audience,*)
  A pirate stands ! Him whom I sought,
If so *he'll* give me certain thanks,
  Because I've praised him as I ought.
Alas, it is no use to ask,
To hide his name is e'er his task.

(*Enter* PHIL. *who advances to foot lights.*)

PHIL.  I asked of the drama,
          Is this good ?
      I asked of ourselves,
          Are we content ?
      I asked of my stanzas,
          Are you rhyme ?
      I asked of the audience,
          Are you pleased ?
      Did the drama agree ?
          Ah no !
      Did we answer ourselves ?
          Ah me !
      Did my stanzas rhyme ?
          Utterly no !
      Did the audience assent ?
          Alas !

(*Enter* PEN. *who advances to foot-lights.*)

PEN.  You've heard the scanty pros and
        Know the dreary cons, and now
      You'll see more fully why
        We did this play. I shall not feel
        Content, nor pleased at all,
        Unless I know you'd try,
      To understand our basis well, and all
        Our premiss fair, and then you'd
            Clearly see
      The ground-work of our feelings, I mean
        The cause of our emotions,
            And there'd be
        Some germs of pity in your minds,
        And you would not rashly blame,
            Our parts, and now
      I beg you'll draw conclusions just, or
        Rather in this case I'll stretch
        A point and as you know,

That you should reason leniently, more
    Tenderly than well,
Else I should fear to ask for smiles to show
  The conclusion that you tell,
    My conscience pricks me just a little
For rational or sound
    We've hardly been,
I've tried to keep them to the point,
  But I'm afraid the point
Has ne'er been seen,
But if, Oh, audience, for yourselves
  In wasting thus your time,
    You should strong pity feel,
    I pray you hide it, remembering
The shame, the reasoning ones
In our poor caste are trying to conceal.

CAPTAIN DELAVILLE, DIANA, CHERUBINA, MEDORA, PHILLIDA, PENELOPE.

## Curtain.

Printed by Libri Plureos GmbH in Hamburg, Germany